The Snow Queen

First published in English in 1991 by Floris Books
15 Harrison Gardens, Edinburgh
© 1990 Verlag J F Schreiber, Postfach 285, Esslingen, Germany
English version © Floris Books 1991
British Library CIP Data available   ISBN 0-86315-128-0
Printed in Spain

Hans Christian Andersen

The Snow Queen

A Fairy Tale in Seven Stories
Illustrated by Anastasiya Archipova

Floris Books

The Snow Queen

A fairy tale in seven stories

First story: The looking glass and the broken bits

The story starts with a wicked imp, one of the wickedest of them all!
One day he was in a very good humour. He had made a looking-glass
with the magic power of making anything good and beautiful that
looked into it shrink to nothing, while everything bad and ugly
simply grew even worse. If they looked in it, even the nicest people
became so nasty you wouldn't recognize them. This was great fun,
thought the wicked imp.

All the other imps said that for the first time, you could see what
human beings really looked like. They ran about all over the world
with the looking-glass, doing mischief everywhere.

Then the imps thought they would fly up to Heaven and make fun
of the angels. But the higher they flew with the looking-glass, the
harder it was for them to hold on to it. As they flew higher and
higher, all at once the looking-glass shot out of their hands and
crashed to earth, where it broke into billions of pieces of glass.

Now this caused even more mischief than before; for many of the
bits were smaller than a grain of sand, and these all went flying round
the world. As each tiny splinter had the same power as the whole
looking-glass, if it got into someone's eyes, it would stick there and

make them have an eye only for what was bad. And if anyone got a little bit in their hearts, that was really dreadful, for then their hearts became like a lump of ice. Larger pieces of glass were used to make spectacles which made everything go wrong when people put them on. The wicked imp laughed till his sides split. Meanwhile millions of little bits went on floating in the air. Now listen to what happened to one of them.

Second Story: A little boy and a little girl

In the middle of the city, there lived two poor children who loved each other like brother and sister. He was called Kay and she was called Gerda. They lived in next-door houses with their rooms under the eaves. A little window opened out from each gable. You only had to step across in order to get from one window to the other.

Here where the parents had a little roof garden with rose-bushes, the children would sit together on summer days, reading or playing happily. In winter, they played indoors. The attic windows would often be quite frozen; then they would warm pennies by the stove and, pressing them on the glass, make little peepholes to look out at the falling snow.

"That's the swarming of the white bees," said Granny.

"Have they a queen bee as well?" asked Kay.

"Why, yes!" said Granny. "She flies with the swarm! On winter nights she peeps in at the windows, and then they freeze up all strangely, just like flowers."

"Yes, we've seen it!" cried the two children.

"Can the Snow Queen come inside?" asked the little girl. "Just let her come," said the boy, "and I'll put her on the hot stove and make her melt." But Granny smoothed his hair and told them other stories.

One winter's evening, Kay climbed up to the window and peeped out. Snow was falling and a large snowflake came to rest on the edge of the roof. The snowflake grew and grew until Kay saw it was a woman, dressed in the finest gauze, made up of millions of starry flakes. She herself was so pretty and delicate, yet was made of glittering ice. Her eyes gazed like bright stars, never still or resting. She nodded to him and waved her hand. At that, Kay was frightened and jumped down.

A few days later, Kay and Gerda were looking at a picture-book when — just as the clock in the church tower struck five — Kay said: "Oh, something pricked me! And now I've got something in my eye!"

Gerda put her arms round him and looked closely while he blinked; but no, there was nothing to be seen.

"I think it's gone!" Kay said. But it hadn't. It was a tiny splinter of glass from the wicked imp's looking-glass. Poor Kay had a bit right in his heart; soon it would be like a lump of ice.

"Why are you crying?" he asked impatiently. "It makes you look ugly! There's nothing wrong with me!"

When Gerda showed him the book again, Kay said it was babyish. He seemed so different, Gerda hardly knew him.

The next day, Kay appeared carrying his sledge. He shouted to Gerda: "I'm allowed to go and sledge on the square with the other boys!" And with that he was off.

The boys were all playing on the square when along came a big white sleigh. The person driving it was wrapped in a white fur cloak and cap. As the sleigh drove slowly round, Kay tied his sledge to the back for fun — like the older boys did — and was pulled along. Faster and faster it went, the driver turning round and giving Kay a nod as if they knew each other. They drove out through the city gates. And then the snow began falling so fast that Kay couldn't see in front of him as they tore along. He tried to loose the rope from the sleigh, but it was of no use; his sledge was tied fast and travelling like the wind. He shouted; but the sleigh only went racing on.

Then all at once the sleigh stopped, and the driver got up. It was a lady, tall, straight and all gleaming white. It was the Snow Queen.

"Why, you're cold!" she said. "Come, wrap yourself in my bearskin cloak!"

She sat him beside her in the big white sleigh, and put her cloak round him; it felt like sinking in a snowdrift.

"Do you still feel cold?" she asked, kissing him on the forehead. Her kiss was colder than ice and went straight to his heart, which was already half ice. The Snow Queen kissed Kay once more, and by this time he had forgotten little Gerda and everyone at home.

They flew over woods and lakes, over seas and lands. The cold wind whistled and the snow glittered; up above the moon shone clear and Kay watched it all the long winter's night. During the day he slept at the Snow Queen's feet.

Third Story: The woman who worked magic

Spring came round at last, bringing warmer sunshine.

"Kay's dead and gone!" said little Gerda to the swallows.

"We don't think so!" they all said.

"I'm going to put on my new red shoes," she said. "And then I'll go and ask the river!" Early next morning, she put on her red shoes and went through the city gate and down to the river.

"Have you taken my playmate, Kay?" she asked. "I'll give you my new shoes if you'll return him to me!"

The waves seemed to nod so strangely to her that she took her shoes and threw them into the river, but they floated straight back. She thought she hadn't thrown the shoes far enough and so, climbing to the end of a boat which lay there, she threw the shoes out again. The boat wasn't tied up, and it started to float away from the bank.

Although Gerda was quite frightened, she thought to herself: "Perhaps the river will take me to Kay!" And cheered by this she stood up and gazed at the beautiful green banks. In time she came by a curious little thatched house with two wooden soldiers outside.

Gerda called out and an old, old woman came from the house, leaning on a crooked stick.

"You poor child!" said the old woman. "However did you come to be drifting away into the wide, wide world?" And hooking her crooked stick on to the boat, she pulled it ashore and lifted Gerda out. And Gerda was glad to be on dry land, though a bit afraid of the strange old woman.

Then Gerda told her story, and asked the old woman if she had seen little Kay, and the woman said no, but he was sure to come; meanwhile, she should cheer up and must taste her cherries, and enjoy her lovely flower-garden. And while Gerda was eating her cherries, the old woman combed her hair with a golden comb till it curled and shone.

"How I've longed for a little girl like you!" said the old woman. "Now just you see how well we two are going to get on!" And as her hair was combed, Gerda forgot all about Kay; for the old woman could work magic, though she wasn't a wicked witch. She simply wished to keep little Gerda with her.

Time passed, and soon Gerda was allowed into the garden to enjoy the flowers in the warm sunshine. The most beautiful of all was a rose-bush. One day Gerda sat by it and, thinking of the lovely roses at home in the roof garden, she remembered Kay.

"Oh, I must find Kay!" cried Gerda. "Do you think he's dead and gone?" she asked the roses.

"He isn't dead!" they said. "We were in the ground all winter. That's where the dead are, but Kay wasn't there!"

Gerda ran to the garden gate and shook the rusty latch till it came loose and the gate sprang open. And then Gerda ran in her bare feet into the wide world. At last she couldn't run any longer and sat down on a big stone.

"Why, it's autumn already! Oh, dear, how I've wasted my time!" said Gerda. "Now I daren't rest!" And she got up to go.

Fourth Story: The prince and princess

Gerda travelled on for what seemed a very long time. One day as she rested, a big crow hopped in front of her. It wagged its head, and said: "Caw! Caw!" Gerda told the crow her story and asked if it had seen Kay.

The crow said thoughtfully: "Perhaps I have. It may be Kay! But I rather think he's forgotten you now for the princess!"

"Does he live with a princess?" asked Gerda.

"Why, yes!" said the crow. "In this kingdom lives a princess who's very clever. She was sitting on the throne last week when she thought: 'Why shouldn't I get married?'

"She told her ladies in waiting, and they were all delighted. They declared that any handsome young man was free to come and talk to

the princess, and the one who talked best would be her husband. Well," said the crow, "people flocked to the palace."

"But Kay?" asked Gerda. "Was he among them?"

"Hold on! I'm coming to that! Yesterday a little fellow came marching up. His eyes shone like yours and he had lovely long hair, but poor clothes."

"That was Kay!" cried Gerda, delighted. "And he won the princess?"

"She thought he talked the best," said the crow.

"Why, of course it was Kay," said Gerda. "He is so clever. Oh, please will you take me to the palace?"

"A child with bare feet will never be admitted," said the crow. "But don't despair. My sweetheart knows a secret way in. Wait here," said the crow, and flew off.

At nightfall, the crow returned with his sweetheart. They went into the palace garden, and the crows took Gerda to a little back door and up the stairs. At last they were in a bedchamber, where there were two beds shaped like lilies. One of them was white, and here lay the princess. In the other there lay a young man. Yes, it was Kay! She called his name and held up a lamp. He woke, turned, and — it wasn't Kay. The prince only resembled Kay, being young and handsome.

Waking in her white bed, the princess asked what was the matter. And little Gerda wept and told her story and what the crows had done for her.

"You poor thing," they said. And the prince got up and let Gerda sleep in his bed, she looked so very weary.

The next day she was dressed all in silk and velvet, with warm boots and a muff. A coach of pure gold stood at the door, full of sugar

biscuits, fruit and ginger-nuts. The prince and the princess helped her into the carriage and wished her good luck.

"Goodbye!, Goodbye!" they cried, and the crows flew up into a tree, and flapped their black wings as long as the coach was in sight.

Fifth Story: The little robber girl

They drove through the dark forest, where the golden coach shone like fire and caught the robbers' eyes.

"Gold! Gold!" they cried; rushing forward, they seized the horses, killed the coachman and then pulled little Gerda out of the coach.

"She's plump, she's been fattened on nuts!" said an old robber woman, drawing out her sharp knife. Then suddenly she cried out for she had been bitten by her own daughter, who was as wild and mischievous as anything.

"She'll play with me," cried the little robber girl. "I want to go in the coach with her." And she got her own way, she was so spoilt and self-willed. She and Gerda got in and away they drove. The little robber girl was the same age as Gerda but stronger and dark-skinned. With her arm round Gerda, she said: "I suppose you're a princess."

"No," said Gerda, and she told her all her adventures.

The robber girl looked at her and said: "They shan't kill you; I'll see that I do it myself." And drying Gerda's eyes, she put her hands into the warm muff.

The coach soon arrived at the robbers' castle. In the big hall, soup was simmering over a large fire, and meat was turning on spits.

"You shall sleep here with me and all my pets!" said the robber girl. They ate and drank, and then went into a corner, where there were blankets and straw. Up above there were nearly a hundred pigeons sleeping.

"They're all mine," said the robber girl. "And this is my old Baa-baa!" She tugged the horn of a reindeer, which was tied up. "Every night I tickle his neck with my knife; that frightens him!"

And she ran her knife over the reindeer's neck. The poor creature backed in fear, but the girl only laughed.

"Now," said the robber girl, "tell me again about Kay."

So Gerda told her again while two wood pigeons in a cage went on cooing above. Then the robber girl put her arms round Gerda and fell fast asleep. But Gerda couldn't sleep a wink, not knowing if she would live or die.

All at once the wood-pigeons called: "Coo! Coo! We've seen little Kay. He was in the Snow Queen's carriage."

"What's that?" cried Gerda. "Where did they go?"

"They went towards Lapland, where there's always snow."

"Oh, Kay, Kay!" sighed Gerda, as she lay sleepless.

In the morning Gerda told the robber girl what the wood-pigeons had said, and she looked very serious, but then asked the reindeer: "Do you know where Lapland is?"

"I was born there," said the animal, its eyes sparkling.

The robber girl said: "I love tickling you with my knife. But I'll let you go, so you can take this little girl to the Snow Queen's palace."

The reindeer leapt for joy. The robber girl lifted Gerda up, tied her fast and even gave her a little cushion.

"Take my mother's big mittens," she said, "for it will be cold. Hands in!"

Stretching out her hands in the big mittens to the robber girl, Gerda said good-bye, and the reindeer flew off through the forest and over swamps and plains for all it was worth. And soon they were in Lapland.

Sixth Story: The Lapp woman and the Finn woman

They came to a stop at a wretched little house where there was nobody but an old Lapp woman frying fish at an oil-lamp. The reindeer told her Gerda's whole story as Gerda was too cold to speak.

"Oh, you poor things!" said the Lapp woman. "You've got hundreds of miles to go yet, right into Finnmark. I'll write a note on a piece of dried cod for you to take to the Finn woman. She'll tell you more than I can!"

And so when Gerda had eaten and warmed up, the Lapp woman wrote a few words on a piece of dried cod, tied Gerda on to the reindeer again, and off it sprang. The loveliest blue Northern Lights burnt all night long. And so they came to Finnmark, where they knocked at the Finn woman's chimney, for she didn't have a door.

Inside it was so hot that the Finn woman herself wore few clothes. She was a little woman, and rather grubby. She took off Gerda's mittens and boots, read the message on the dried cod three times and put the fish in the cooking-pot. Then she drew the reindeer aside and whispered:

"Little Kay is with the Snow Queen sure enough, and there he is perfectly content. But that's because he's got a splinter of glass in his heart and another in his eye. They'll have to come out, or he'll never be human again and the Snow Queen will have him in her power."

"Can't you give Gerda something, so that she'll have power, too."

"I can't give her any greater power than she already has! Don't you see how well she has got on in the world, in her bare feet? It's in her heart! She's a sweet and innocent child. If she can't find her way to the Snow Queen and get the glass out of little Kay, then we can't help her! Ten miles from here is the edge of the Snow Queen's garden; leave the little girl by the berry bush there." So saying the Finn woman lifted Gerda on to the reindeer, which ran off as fast as its legs would carry it.

"Oh, I didn't get my boots! I didn't get my mittens!" cried Gerda. She could feel the biting cold. But the reindeer ran on till it came to the Snow Queen's garden. There it kissed Gerda while tears rolled down the creature's cheeks. Then it left poor Gerda there, without shoes, without gloves, in the middle of dreadful, icy-cold Finnmark.

She ran on, and soon met a whole regiment of snowflakes; but they didn't fall from the sky. They were running, and the nearer they came the bigger they grew: they were the Snow Queen's sentries!

Now Gerda said her prayers. The cold was so fierce that she could see her own breath like a cloud of smoke; denser and denser it grew, until it took the form of bright little angels that went on growing. Every one wore a helmet and carried a sword and a shield. More and more came, until there was a whole army. And they set about the snowflakes and broke them into a hundred pieces, allowing Gerda to walk safely on. And the angels stroked her feet and hands, so that she didn't feel the cold as she walked on to the Snow Queen's palace.

Seventh Story: What happened in the Snow Queen's palace

The palace walls were of drifting snow, the windows and doors of cutting winds. There were over a hundred halls; the biggest stretched for many miles. All were lit up by the fierce Northern Lights, and were so large, so empty, so icy-cold. Here, Kay was quite blue with cold; though he never felt it. His heart was as a lump of ice. The Snow Queen had flown off to touch the mountains up with white, and Kay sat all by himself in the bare hall, stiff and silent.

Then Gerda entered the palace, through the big gates of biting winds. There she saw Kay. She knew him at once and flung her arms round his neck, holding him tight and crying: "Kay! Dear Kay!"

But he sat perfectly still and stiff and cold. Seeing this, Gerda shed hot tears and they fell on his breast and went through to his heart, where they melted the lump of ice and swallowed up the glass splinter. Then Kay burst into tears; and wept till the bit of glass fell out of his eye, when he knew her again and cried for joy:

"Gerda! Dear Gerda! Where have you been all this long time? And where have I been?"

Then, looking round him, he said: "How cold and bare it is!" And he held Gerda tight while she cried and laughed for joy. Then Gerda

kissed his cheeks and they became rosy. She kissed his eyes and they shone like hers; she kissed his hands and feet and he was well and strong.

And taking each other by the hand, they walked out of the big hall. They talked of home, of Granny and the roses in the roof garden, and wherever they went, the winds dropped and the sun broke through. And when they got to the berry bush, there waiting for them was the reindeer which carried Kay and Gerda first to the Finn woman's where they warmed themselves, and then to the Lapp woman who had got ready her sledge.

The reindeer ran alongside as far as the country's border; there, where the first green things peeped up from the ground, they said goodbye. And the birds began to sing, the wood was in bud and there on a splendid horse came a young girl with a red cap on her head and

pistols in front. It was the little robber girl who was tired of staying at home. She knew Gerda at once and Gerda knew her. They were delighted. And taking them both by the hands, she promised that if ever she visited their town she would call and see them. And with that she rode off into the wide world.

Kay and Gerda went on hand in hand and everywhere were flowers and everything green. The church bells were ringing as they came to their own town. And they walked into the house where everything stood where it had stood before, Granny sat reading from the Bible and the clock still said "Tick! Tick!" But as they walked in at the door they felt that they had become grown-up people. Now Kay and Gerda had forgotten, like a bad dream, the cold empty splendour at the Snow Queen's palace. The roses were blooming by the open windows, and it was summer, warm and blessed summer.